Getting Started:

Clicking

with Your Rabbit

Joan Orr and Teresa Lewin

Photo credits:
From B.U.N.S, Bunnies Urgently Needing Shelter, Santa Clara Humane Society,
California:
    Heidi Bratt: 1, 3, 7, 15, 17, 21, 25, 30, 35, 39, 51, 64 a, b, 71
    Bill Hepp: 49, 78
    Jean Silva: 11, 31

Joan Orr: Front cover, 4, 20, 23, 36, 38, 43, 44, 46, 53, 55, 57, 70

Other titles in this series
Getting Started: Clicker Training for Dogs by Karen Pryor
Getting Started: Clicker Training for Cats by Karen Pryor
Getting Started: Clicker Training for Horses by Alexandra Kurland
Getting Started: Clicker Training for Birds by Melinda Johnson

Getting Started: Clicking with Your Rabbit
© 2006 Joan Orr and Teresa Lewin

For information contact:
Karen Pryor Clickertraining
49 River Street, Ste. #3
Waltham, MA 02453
781-398-0754
www.clickertraining.com

Library of Congress Control Number 2006924593

ISBN 978-1-890948-23-8

Book design by Codesign, Boston

Printed in the United States of America

10 9 8 7 6 5 4 3 2 1

A
Karen Pryor

Clicker
Book

Getting Started:

Clicking
with Your Rabbit

Joan Orr and Teresa Lewin

Karen Pryor
Clickertraining

Contents

CHAPTER 1
What? Train a Rabbit?

Rabbits ... furry and lovable, of course; quirky and silly, sometimes; full of energy and mischief, undoubtedly. But trainable? You bet! You're probably training your rabbit without even realizing it. Is he litter box trained? Does he come to see you when you go to his cage? Then you've already taken your first steps toward training.

There's so much more your rabbit can learn! Have you ever seen a rabbit fetch? Or play basketball? (Rabbit-sized, of course.) What about navigating a course of jumps and tunnels? These are all tricks you can teach your pet bunny. You can also teach him some tricks to make your life together easier. How would you like it if your rabbit sat still while you

What! Train a rabbit? Of course you can!

trimmed his nails or came when you called his name? All it takes is a little training.

Training is actually good for your rabbit. When it is all positive—rewards only and no punishment—training can replace many of the activities and thinking that rabbits do naturally in the wild. Finding food, creating homes, and staying safe all require various activities and problem solving; most of these things are not required of a pet living in a cage or a human house. Training sessions provide your pet with mental and physical stimulation, and allow him to use his natural abilities. This will contribute to a longer and happier life for your rabbit.

Many rabbits languish in their cages most of their lives, but your trained bunny will delight you with tricks and antics. You will be eager to take him out of his cage and explore further possibilities—and he will be eager to explore them with you.

This positive method of training is popularly known as clicker training, and it is a great way to teach your rabbit all sorts of things. Clicker training is fun for both you and your bunny and helps to strengthen the bond between you. According to clicker training pioneer Karen Pryor, "Clicking with rabbits brightens their lives, exercises their surprisingly lively minds, and brings out their endearing personalities. They'll love training you to click and treat! It's easy to learn, and mentally and physically enriching for pets and their owners."

CLICKER TRAINING DEFINED

What exactly is clicker training? It is a teaching system in which a click sound is used to tell the rabbit he has done the right thing. The click sound is made by using a small, handheld device that clicks when pressed. The sound the clicker makes when you press it tells your rabbit, "Yes! That's right!" The click is always followed closely with a food treat so that your pet comes to associate the click with something good. Soon the rabbit wants to hear the click sound. This is because he knows a treat will follow and this makes him feel happy and secure.

Clicker training teaches the bunny that he can cause you to click, and then give him a treat, through his own actions. Let's say, for example, that you click and treat each time he comes toward you in his cage. Soon he will actively try to get you to click by coming toward you when you come near the cage. Next you will be able to add a verbal cue (a command) and your bunny will start coming to you when you call. "It's very exciting to see an animal

When the rabbit hears the click sound he knows a treat will follow, which makes him feel happy and secure.

experience the 'Aha!' moment when he suddenly realizes that he can actively control the clicker game," said Pryor.

Any treat that you can give to your rabbit that he desires and that motivates him to repeat a behavior is called a reinforcer. A treat can be food, petting, freedom, or a chance to play with a favorite toy. Food treats are the strongest reinforcers for most rabbits, and we recommend that you begin training your rabbit with food treats.

In clicker training, you influence a pet's behavior in two ways. The first is positive reinforcement, in which you reward your pet with a click and treat when he does something you like and want him to do again. The other way you influence behavior is simply to ignore behavior that you don't like. Behavior that is reinforced will become stronger; behavior that is ignored tends to fade away. Punishment, scolding, or physical correction are not used in clicker training.

CLICKER TRAINING BASICS

In clicker training, you:
- Reward desired behavior
- Ignore unwanted behavior
- Do not use punishment, scolding, or physical correction

You may be wondering, "Why do I need the clicker? Why can't I just give my rabbit a treat without the click sound? Why can't I just say 'good boy' to my bunny rather than clicking?"

We click because the sound is clear, consistent, and precise. A word can be spoken in different ways. An animal may not recognize the same word if spoken in a different tone. The rabbit knows that the click means a treat is coming, every time.

A click can be made at exactly the same time the animal does the behavior we want to reward. It is difficult to say a word at precisely the same moment as the behavior; usually a spoken word comes a moment later. When the click occurs at the same instant as the behavior, the rabbit knows exactly what he did to deserve a treat. It is not usually possible to deliver a treat exactly at the same time a behavior occurs, especially if your rabbit is in a cage or across the room from you.

The click lets you "mark" the desired behavior exactly,

Angel gets clicks and treats for exploring her new play house.

telling your rabbit: "This is what you are doing that will earn you a treat." If you simply give a treat, the rabbit may have done several other behaviors by the time he actually receives the treat. He may then be confused about which behavior or which aspect of the behavior resulted in the treat, and therefore will not know what behavior to repeat in order to earn another treat.

For example, perhaps you are trying to teach your bunny to come to the door of the cage. He has done so, but by the time you open the door to give the food reward, the bunny has already become frustrated and started chewing on the door. You give the treat because the bunny came to the door, but he associates the reward with chewing on the door. You may have inadvertently taught your rabbit to chew on his cage door to get a treat. If you use the clicker to instantly "mark" the appropriate behavior of coming to the door, then he will learn that the correct behavior is to come to the door of the cage. You will be amazed by how smart your bunny is! All he needs is to be able to communicate effectively with you, and you with him. The clicker makes this possible.

CLICKER TRAINING WORKS

There are hundreds of thousands of clicker trainers around the world, training almost every conceivable captive species. Why? Because clicker training works! It works with dolphins and birds that you've seen in trained animal shows. It works with search-and-rescue dogs. It works with elephants and tigers, and even with turtles and fish.

Clicker training is also making a difference in the lives of shelter animals waiting for adoption. Many animal shelters have begun clicker training with their rabbits, dogs, and ferrets.

Andrea Bratt Frick and Jean Silva of B.U.N.S. (Bunnies Urgently Needing Shelter) in California have been clicker training shelter rabbits to enrich their lives and make them more adoptable. Jean Silva says, "Once you get started and learn how to use the clicker, you and your rabbit become 'hooked.' It is simple to use, and the results are so powerful! We have been using the clicker to get all our bunnies to come to the front of their cages to appear friendly to help them become more adoptable. Also, we have taught them little tricks such as 'Gimme Ten' so that the bunnies (who were fearful at first) would interact with potential adopters."

Anyone Can Train a Rabbit

Who are all these clicker trainers? They are people just like you. Some are adults, some are kids, some are professional trainers, and some are shelter volunteers. Anyone who can press a clicker and give a pet a treat can clicker train. Sometimes beginners train in teams, with one person clicking and the other treating. This is a good way for new clicker trainers to learn because one person focuses on handling the animal and pressing the clicker, and the other on delivering the treat quickly.

All Rabbits Can Be Trained

We have yet to encounter a rabbit that cannot be clicker trained. Some rabbits learn more quickly, some will work for longer periods, and some get bored easily. Any rabbit that can be motivated by something you have that he wants can be clicker trained. Sometimes it takes a bunny a few sessions to get used to the sound of the clicker or to associate the click with the treat. Some pets catch on right away. We have trained many rabbits, and even within this one species there is a wide range of ability when it comes to learning new things.

The key to success with clicker training a rabbit is to understand your rabbit. Observe to see what he likes to eat, what kinds of behaviors he does naturally, and what kind of environment he prefers. Consult the resources listed in Chapter 8 (see page 79) to find out what others have observed about rabbits. You will want to know what type of home your rabbit likes, what toys and activities he prefers, how to keep him healthy, and what kinds of treats you can use for training. A wonderful aspect of clicker training your bunny is the time that you spend observing and playing with him. Once you understand what makes your bunny tick you can set up your training sessions to ensure success.

Bunnies can learn a lot! This clicker-trained bunny has learned to "weave" through a line of "carrot sticks" the way agility-trained dogs go through the weave pole obstacle.

CHAPTER 2

Getting Started

Clicker training is based on the observation that behaviors that are rewarded happen more frequently. In clicker training, you don't worry about correcting mistakes. Instead, you reward the "right" behavior. The clicker makes it easy for the animal to understand what behavior is desired, and to connect his exhibition of that behavior with the tasty reward.

The basic steps of clicker training are very simple:

1. Get your rabbit to do the behavior you want.

2. Click the instant he does it.

3. Reward your rabbit with a treat he loves.

4. Add a cue (command) so that the rabbit knows the name of the behavior you want him to perform.

5. Gradually phase out ("fade," in clicker training terminology) the clicker and treats so that the rabbit will do his tricks even if you don't have a treat.

TOOLS OF THE TRADE

To begin clicker training, you need to gather a few training tools. These include a clicker, treats, and some training props. You also will need a place to train. Let's look at the tools individually.

The Clicker

The first thing you will need to get started with clicker training is a clicker. These can be purchased at many stores where dog training supplies are sold and online at **www.clickertraining.com** and in Canada at **www.doggonecrazy.ca**. Some clickers are quieter, some make different types of sounds, and some are easier to press, so you might want to try out different types.

If you have a shy animal or you have difficulty with your hands, a quiet clicker, the i-Click, may be a better choice than the louder box clicker. On the other hand, if you want your pet to hear the clicker at a distance or in a loud room, the louder box clicker may be better. Yet another clicker, the Clicker+, makes four different sounds, which may be useful if you want to use a different sound for different pets working at the same time. (Until you get the hang of clicker training, however, it may be best to begin training your pets individually.)

The objective in introducing the clicker is to have the rabbit understand that click means treat, so you next need to find out what kind of treats to use.

Treats

Rabbits are like people: Different individuals have different favorite foods. To find out which treats are your rabbit's favorites, offer him several different foods and treats in a bowl at mealtime. See which ones he eats first. Try to discern the top two or three favorites. Repeat this process for several days until all the different foods that your rabbit might like have been tried. At the last test meal, offer all the top two or three favorites at once and from this identify the absolute top three.

Because some bunnies will most enjoy foods that they shouldn't have too much of, it is a good idea to find out which nutritious foods are among the favorites. For example, rabbits usually love raisins, but more than two or three per day would not be good for your pet because the sugar content is so high. Find out what your rabbit's favorite green vegetable is; you can feed him much more of this food in one session. Processed foods like crackers or sugary cereal are not good for rabbits at all, but un-sugared shredded wheat makes a healthy treat.

Use common sense and moderation and try to avoid sudden drastic changes to your rabbit's diet. If you use a commercial mixed feed, watch to see which items from this your rabbit prefers; pick out his favorites for use in training and give him the remainder for regular meals.

A good training treat is small or can be broken up into tiny pieces that your pet can eat quickly without having to do a lot of chewing or searching around for dropped crumbs. A larger treat, such as a carrot or a piece of lettuce that you can hold while your rabbit bites off a piece, also works well to deliver a reward quickly in small amounts.

You may have heard that some dog trainers withhold food for the whole day before a training class so that their dogs will be hungry at class time. We don't recommend this for rabbits (or for dogs either) because it can have disastrous effects on the intestinal workings of your bunny. Pets that

Max is learning to "sit pretty." As he reaches upwards he lifts his paws, and hears the click. Then he gets a small piece of a favorite treat. Soon he will lift his paws on purpose to earn a click.

are so hungry as to be frantic to get food are not able to focus for fun and stress-free learning. Rabbits need to eat almost constantly to keep their digestive tract functioning properly. So provide hay and water in your bunny's cage at all times, and use the food pellets as training treats.

Small rabbits need a quarter cup of pellets for a full day's feeding. Use that quarter cup and spread it out throughout the day for training treats. You can supplement this with some other favorite treats you have identified. Pre-measure small amounts so that you don't get carried away and give too many sweet treats.

Some rabbits are finicky and they may like a certain food one day and not care for it the next. It is a good idea, therefore, to have several different foods available for training in each session and mix them up so that you don't end up with a bunny that refuses to cooperate unless you are offering peeled grapes.

WHAT TO FEED YOUR RABBIT

Hay should be your rabbit's main food source, supplemented with pellets, fruits, and vegetables. Healthy, recommended treats:

Fresh veggies (2 cups per 6 pounds body weight, per day):

Carrots (2–4 inches of carrot maximum per day)

Carrot, beet, and radish tops

Celery (remove the strings)

Mustard or collard greens

Cilantro

Clover

Dandelion flowers and leaves

Parsley

Brussels sprouts

Green peppers

Broccoli (leaves and stems)

Alfalfa, radish, and clover sprouts

Romaine lettuce (not iceberg)

Rabbit food timothy pellets (1/4–1/2 cup per 6 pounds body weight per day)

OKAY IN SMALL AMOUNTS:

Raisins (two or three per day)

Fresh fruit (up to 2 ounces per 6 pounds body weight per day):
   Apples
   Bananas

Peaches

Grapes

Strawberries

Raspberries

Blueberries

Melon

Orange

Commercial rabbit treats

Spinach

Kale

NOT RECOMMENDED FOR RABBITS:

Processed crackers or cookies

Treats with meat

Seeds and nuts, including apple seeds

Chocolate

High-sugar, high-fat breakfast cereals

Peas

Potatoes

Corn

Iceberg lettuce

You can find out more about feeding baby, juvenile, and senior rabbits at the website of the House Rabbit Society, **www.rabbit.org**.

Props for Tricks

Props, of course, vary from trick to trick. They can be simple—a ball, a margarine container lid to touch—or quite elaborate—rabbit-sized agility equipment including weave poles, jumps, and tunnels. The only real requirement is that the props be bunny-safe. You don't want your pet to chew something dangerous or to have something flimsy fall apart and frighten him.

Two especially helpful props are targets and target sticks. A target is something the bunny has been taught to touch with his nose or foot. A plastic lid or even a Post-it Note® can be a stationary target. A target stick is a moveable target that can be used to guide your bunny through a behavior. We'll look more at targeting in the next chapter, "Ready, Set, Go! ... Your First Trick."

The Training Area

Training sessions should be fun and as stress-free as possible for both you and your rabbit. If your bunny comes out of his cage only to be chased behind the sofa by the cat, and you spend an hour trying to coax him out, your training session won't be particularly fun or productive for anyone (except maybe the cat). By thinking ahead and setting up the environment properly, training sessions can go smoothly and safely. To start, put the cat (or other equally incompatible animal) in another room. Then put a note on the door to remind other family members not to let the cat back in.

Rabbits are prey animals and need to feel comfortable and safe in their surroundings before they can learn and play. If your rabbit is shy or fearful, you can train him in his cage initially. If he is happy to come out of his home, then make arrangements to keep him from escaping by closing doors or creating barriers to keep him in a safe area. The bathroom floor can be an excellent training area if the toilet is closed and the tub is empty. There, bunnies are safe from chewable wires, and there's little to distract them. Put a litter box in each corner to help with litter box training and to give the rabbit a familiar place to go if he gets anxious.

Some rabbits may need more time than others to become sufficiently comfortable to take food in the training area. You may have to sit with your rabbit for a few sessions and let him explore and relax. If you are sure your chosen training area is completely safe, leave your pet in there for a while with a litter box, hay, drinking water, and some toys to become familiar with his surroundings.

If you'd like to be able to take your rabbit to different places to perform his tricks, a portable training area is useful. For small rabbits, a child's portable playpen works well. For

You don't need to be close to the rabbit to clicker train. This rabbit feels safe in a portable exercise pen. He is learning to get on a box for a click and a tossed treat.

larger rabbits, a portable dog exercise pen with non-slip, roll-up matting for the floor works well.

Towels draped over the side of the pen can help the rabbit feel secure and minimize distractions in a new environment. Once your pet gets used to learning new things on the training surface you can take him anywhere and he will feel right at home. Eight-year-old Jennifer and nine-year-old William took their trained bunnies on live television to show off clicker-trained tricks. The bunnies were accustomed to working on a special track while wearing a harness and leash. They weren't at all distracted by the lights and noise of the TV studio because they had their litter boxes, harnesses, and special training surfaces—just like at home.

INTRODUCING THE CLICKER

Okay, you're almost ready to get started with clicker training your rabbit. Before you begin, though, it's important that you give your pet time to get used to the clicker. Some rabbits may find the click sound too loud or may be frightened by it at first. Take care to avoid letting this happen; it's a lot more work to un-frighten a rabbit than it is to introduce the clicker properly and kindly the first time.

Test a new clicker away from your rabbit first to hear how loud or soft it is. The first time you use a clicker with your rabbit, hold the clicker behind your back, or muffle it under your sweater or a cloth. Most rabbits are not bothered by the click sound, so as you progress you may find that you don't need to muffle the sound. Rabbits do have sensitive ears, though, so avoid clicking right beside their ears.

Bring out the clicker for the first time while you are determining which treats are your rabbit's favorites. Click as the rabbit takes a piece of food. Click when you put the food into the cage. When you give the daily hay or extra veggies, click when you put those in as well. Your rabbit will begin to build a positive association between the click sound and the arrival and taste of food. At this point you are not clicking for any particular behavior, but just to get

First the click, timed to match the behavior exactly; then the treat.

your rabbit accustomed to the click and to feel good when he hears the sound.

At this stage of training, you want to avoid clicking for the same behavior every time. For example, if your bunny jumps at the bars in anticipation of food, and you click and then feed every time he jumps, you will have taught him to jump at the bars whenever he sees you. The bunny thinks that jumping at the bars causes the food to arrive, while in fact jumping has nothing to do with whether or not you are going to feed him. This is called superstitious behavior. A rabbit called PG believes that shredding papers in front of the cage door makes it open. Dogs and cats frequently show superstitious behaviors, such as barking in the belief that it will cause the door to open, running to the food bowl and back to cause food to be dispensed, and so on. Avoid creating superstitions by clicking during different types of behaviors while you are still building up the positive association with the clicker. For now, all you want your rabbit to learn is that "click" equals "food."

Once you have identified foods to use in training and have associated the click with feeding in the cage, give your bunny a small treat and click simultaneously. Do this a few times until it seems as if the rabbit shows a reaction to the sound of the clicker. If you click and he flicks his ears, or turns to look at the clicker, or moves toward you expectantly, you know the sound of the click is becoming meaningful to him. (At this point, be certain to keep your rabbit moving during the training session. Sometimes giving clicks and treats to a pet that is sitting still teaches the pet to remain motionless, not a helpful beginning to a training session!)

If your rabbit is too shy to take food from your hand or come out of his cage, just offer the food on the ground and click when the pet takes it. Move your hand closer and closer to the food each time until the rabbit will take the food from near your hand and eventually directly from your hand. You will need to use the most favorite treats at first. If you are trying to convince your bunny to come out of the cage, click and treat first as he looks in the direction of the door, then if he turns his head toward the door, then if he makes any movement toward the door. Click and treat for any improvement in coming toward the door of the cage. With a shy rabbit, or one that has come from a situation of abuse or neglect, it may take several (or many) sessions before he will come out of the cage or take food from your hand. (A bold bunny, on the other hand, may just rush right out. Be prepared in advance in case this happens.)

When your rabbit has become comfortable with the sound of the clicker, you're ready to begin training specific behaviors using the basic steps of clicker training.

GET THE BEHAVIOR

The first step to training a specific behavior is to find a way to get the rabbit to do the behavior so that you can reward him. There are four ways to accomplish this.

Capture a Natural Behavior

Observe your rabbit and click and treat when you see him naturally doing something you would like him to do for a trick, or as part of trick. For example, rabbits often sit up on their hind legs to take a look around. If you click and treat your bunny when he does this, you will notice that he will do this more and more often and may even come up to you and offer the behavior as if to say, "Look what I'm doing. Do you see? May I have a treat?"

Lure with Food

Luring with food is a popular way to get dogs and cats to follow a trainer's hand, but it does not work right away with all rabbits. Rabbits are foraging animals and are not inclined to follow moving food. When your rabbit has learned to take food from your hand and has got the idea that he can get you to click and give him a treat, he may begin to follow the food as you move it away and you can click and treat for that movement. Once the rabbit has learned to follow food, you can use this to get him to go over or around objects or come to a place from which you want him to begin a series of tricks. You will actually have more success training your rabbit if you use the luring method sparingly; the other methods described in this section are better for teaching your rabbit to think for himself.

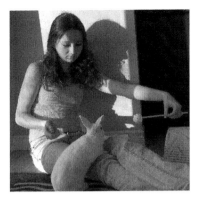

Ann is using a target—a ball on a stick—to teach Angel first to walk and then to jump across her legs.

Follow a Target

You can teach your rabbit to touch a target with his nose and then to follow the target. A good target for a rabbit is a ping-pong ball attached to the end of a stick, although a target can be anything a rabbit learns to touch with his nose or paw. Once the rabbit has learned to follow the target, you can use the target to guide him through an obstacle course or into position to perform other tricks.

Shaping

Once you have the hang of shaping, it can be your most effective method of using clicker training. Shaping is clicking and treating small approximations of the behavior you want, gradually adding more steps until the behavior is complete. For example, to teach your rabbit to come to you, first click when he looks in your direction, then when he turns his head toward you, then when he takes a step, then when he takes two steps, and so on until your rabbit runs toward you hoping for a click and treat. You can use capturing, luring, and targeting to get things started, and then use shaping to perfect the behavior you want.

In most cases you will not be able to train a whole behavior at once. Many behaviors, or tricks, need to be trained in baby steps, which gradually become the whole behavior. For example, if you wanted to teach your bunny to pick up a ball and place it in his bowl, you might first teach him to approach the ball, then to touch the ball with his nose, then to pick up the ball in his mouth, then to drop it in the bowl, and then to carry the ball to the bowl and drop it in.

The important thing is that you make each step easy for your bunny. You want him to be able to succeed frequently so he will be interested in playing the clicker "game." If you expected your bunny to pick up a ball and carry it across the room to his dish on

Picking up a ball, carrying it, and dropping it is a "shaped" behavior. This bunny puts the balls in the white bowl for clicks and treats.

his very first try, you would be setting both yourself and your rabbit up to fail. Start with something he can achieve easily. Perhaps all he has to do is touch the ball with his nose. When he's good at that, add another easy task on top of that one: touch it with his mouth. Then touch it with his mouth open (perhaps wipe something yummy on the ball to encourage him to open his mouth), and then to put his mouth on it.

If he makes a mistake, don't worry about it. Just ignore it. We all make mistakes learning new things! When he figures out what you want, and if he wants the treat, he will do it. If he seems confused, you might need to change something in the environment to make the behavior more likely to occur or work on a simpler version of the behavior.

Don't rush! This isn't a race. Take your time, be patient, and let your bunny have many successes at each level before you move on to a bigger challenge. Remember: When he's successful, you're successful, and that's fun for both of you.

CLICK!

The very instant your bunny does what you want him to do, click. Don't wait for the behavior to be completed. Think of the clicker as if it were a camera, and "take a picture" of the behavior you want by clicking. The click says, "That behavior right there ..." and the treat that follows says, "... I like it. Do it again." The click is a clear yes-or-no signal. When he does what you want, he gets a click. If there's no click, he needs to try something different.

Sometimes you may be too quick as you anticipate your rabbit's movement and you may click by mistake when the rabbit has not actually done the action you intended to click. If you click by mistake, you must still give the treat. Click means treat every time. A few mistakes won't matter in the end if the majority of your clicks are accurate.

REWARD THE BEHAVIOR

Now that your bunny has done what you wanted and been clicked for it, you need to reward him for a job well done. This reward is like a paycheck. Your rabbit learns, "Hey, when I touch that ball, I get a bite of lettuce. I'm going to touch that ball a lot, so I'll get more lettuce!"

Food treats aren't the only rewards you can use. You can choose any reward that your bunny is willing to work for at that moment. What does he want right now? Maybe he wants you to take him out of the cage. Maybe he wants you to pet him. Maybe he wants to play with his favorite toy. Food treats, however, are usually the best rewards for training sessions because they're easy to deliver and much desired by your rabbit.

ADD A CUE

A cue "names" a specific behavior. For example, the verbal word "touch" might tell your rabbit to touch a target with his nose. A particular hand signal might tell your bunny that you want him to "sit pretty". Your rabbit's name might be a cue to come to you. A cue tells your pet that he has an opportunity to earn a reward for doing a specific behavior.

Oreo likes to go over the bridge. When he runs to the bridge to earn a click, Jen will add the cue, "Bridge!"

Add the cue after your animal has figured out what you want and is actively offering the behavior to earn a click and reward. You might wonder, why not use the cue from the beginning? Waiting to add the cue makes learning easier. When you first start teaching a trick, your rabbit has no idea what you want, and because he doesn't speak English, giving the cue won't help him. In fact, it's just noise he has to sort through as he tries to figure out how to earn that click and treat. After he learns the trick, adding the cue makes more sense, because he knows what to do and now has to figure out only when to do it.

Here's how to add a cue:

1. Give the cue just as your rabbit begins to do a behavior that he already knows will earn him a treat. Repeat this sequence of events—cue, behavior/click, and reward—five times.

2. Give the cue a little earlier—just before your rabbit offers the behavior. From now on, click and treat only when your bunny does the behavior after you give the cue. If he offers the behavior when you haven't given the cue, ignore the behavior. Unless the cue comes first, the behavior no longer earns a click and a treat.

3. Finally, use the cue to ask for the behavior at any time, not just when your rabbit was about to offer it on his own.

4. If your rabbit does not succeed three times in a row, then go back to a previous step to avoid frustrating him. You may have to work for several short sessions before he understands that the cue is a signal to perform a behavior.

It's a good idea to add a cue to each of the different behaviors you teach your rabbit. The first cue is the hardest to teach. Once your rabbit understands one cue, subsequent cues will be easier to teach as he gets better and better at applying this concept. Soon he will know what to do to earn a click and a treat, and will be less likely to repeat a favorite behavior as a way to beg for treats. If you establish clear cues for various behaviors, you will amaze and delight friends and family with your clever rabbit and training skills.

The girl's position and her hand signal are the cue for 'kiss.'

FADE THE CLICKER AND TREATS

One of the most common questions people ask about clicker training is, "Will I have to click and treat forever?" The answer is no. The clicker is a communication tool and is used to teach new tricks. When behaviors are well established and your rabbit responds reliably when you give the cue, you can begin to click and treat less often. Choose only the better responses, click and treat intermittently and then only occasionally to keep the behavior strong. Remember, a click means a treat every time— so even when you are trying to fade the clicker, continue to give a treat for every click. Don't be in a rush to stop using the clicker, however. The more often a behavior has been rewarded, the stronger it will become.

If your rabbit forgets his tricks or does not respond to your cues, go back to training again with the clicker and treats until

ENDING A TRAINING SESSION

Your bunny may seem to be having fun playing the clicker game with you, when suddenly he turns his back on you or returns to his cage. Learning new behaviors is fun, but it is also hard work for small animals. They can tire of such concentration.

Don't be discouraged if your bunny leaves the training session. Just allow him to go back to his cage for a rest and try again later. You may have a bunny that eagerly works for only five or six clicks and treats and then ignores you for a while. This is normal. As long as you make a little progress and your rabbit is happy to play even for a short time, consider it a successful session. As you and your bunny become more skilled at clicker training, you will find that he stays with the training for longer and longer. In general, five-minute sessions a few times a day will be more productive than one twenty-minute session.

A good way to control the length of the session is to count out twenty or so treats and when they are gone, the session is over. Once you are familiar with your rabbit's interest level and learning style, you will be able to gauge how many treats to use in a single training session. Try to end each session on a successful note, and give the bunny a small pile of extra pellets as a final reward.

This bonus at the end of a session can signal that you are finished training for now. If your rabbit becomes a clicker addict and you abruptly end a training session by picking up the clicker and leaving, or picking him up and putting him back in his cage, he may feel punished and go into a rabbit sulk.

the former level of performance is reestablished. Clicker trainers call this "going back to kindergarten." You will find that the behavior returns quickly, and often stronger.

You don't always have to click in order to reward your rabbit for a job well done. In fact, offering a reward, especially a non-food reward, at times when you don't click, is a great way to keep the behavior strong as you fade out the clicker. Examples of non-food rewards include a scratch behind the ears, play, and "life rewards" such as opening the cage door when your bunny wants out. Observe your rabbit to learn all the things he likes, and then you'll almost always have a way to reward him when he does something you like.

CHAPTER 3

Ready, Set, Go! ... Your First Trick

Your rabbit feels safe and comfortable in the training environment. You know his favorite food treats and have taught him that the click means great things for bunnies! Now you're ready to train him. Begin with an easy trick that can be used to teach many others: touching a target.

The goal of this behavior is to teach your rabbit to touch a specific object, the target, with his nose. Once the bunny reliably touches a target and then follows the target, you can direct him from place to place and teach him various other things. Target training first requires a suitable target, something large enough for the pet to see. The target can be your hand or any object you hold in your hand or place in the rabbit's training area. A margarine container lid works well for a bunny. If your pet is on the ground and you don't want to bend over, you can attach a target (a lid or maybe a ping-pong ball) to the end of a wooden dowel or even a long-handled wooden spoon. This is also useful if your pet is in a pen and you want to stay out of the pen, or if your rabbit bites and you want to keep your hands out of reach.

BASIC TARGET TRAINING
The following steps are a guide to teaching your rabbit to touch a target. Once your rabbit has learned to touch the

target, you can add the cue so he will perform the behavior when you want him to.

Touch the target

1. Place the target on the ground near the rabbit. Rabbits are foragers and are more likely to investigate something on the ground than something in your hand. Don't push the target close up to your bunny's face, as this may offend him and cause him to avoid the target. Click and treat when he wanders near the target. Each time the rabbit goes near, click and treat. Wait until your pet comes slightly closer to the object with each repetition to win a click and treat.

   If your rabbit does not go near the object, then try this exercise in a smaller area where there is less space to move around and fewer activity choices, or introduce the target in his cage at first. The rabbit will investigate a new object

These bunnies are enjoying being outdoors at an animal shelter in California, but they come running when they see their target, so it's easy to bring them back indoors.

in his home. Eventually the rabbit will touch the object on purpose or by accident. Try to click exactly when that touch happens. Give a most favorite treat for this first touch and for the next few touches. Deliver the treat away from the target so that the rabbit must return to the target to get another click and treat.

2. When your rabbit reliably touches the target, hearing the click and returning to you for a treat each time, move the target an inch or so to a different spot on the ground. Repeat several times.

3. When he touches the target even after it's been moved, hold the target in your hand, moving it slightly each time, and repeat the steps. Hold the target to the side and not right in front of the rabbit, because rabbits' eyes are on the sides of their heads and they do not see things that are too close in front of them.

Touch the target on cue

4. You can now begin to add the cue:
   • Say "Touch" as the rabbit touches the target, and click and treat for the touch.
   • Present the target at various locations a few inches away from the rabbit, say "Touch" as he touches the target, and click and treat for the touch.

Max is learning to follow a target through the weave poles, a typical obstacle for dog agility competition.

- Say "Touch" as you present the target, but before the rabbit touches it. Click and treat for the touch. Repeat three times.
- Try giving the cue before the rabbit moves to touch the target and wait to see if he responds. If not, go back to a previous successful point in the training sequence and do a few more repetitions.

FREQUENTLY ASKED QUESTIONS

How long should I train at one time?

You may be able to click and treat ten or more times. You may get to click and treat only two or three times. Either is fine. Even two or three clicks and treats in a session will help teach your bunny what you want him to do.

My rabbit wanders off after one or two touches. Is there something wrong?

You may find that your rabbit suddenly wanders off after one or two successful touches. This isn't unusual. Rabbits commonly wander away and come back several times during a training session. If he wanders off in the middle of a session, just wait for him to come back, or end the session and try again later.

My bunny doesn't want the treat. What should I do?

Sometimes a rabbit does not come to get the treat each time, or comes to get it and then does not take it. Don't despair, and don't follow him to try to get him to take the treat. Just offer another opportunity for a click. If he refuses the treat twice in a row, try a different treat, or end the training session and try again later.

How can I improve my clicker skills?

Clicking at the instant your rabbit touches the target (or performs any behavior you are training) is a skill that needs practice, but it gets easier and easier. The more accurate your clicks are, the faster your bunny will get the idea that touching the target wins him a treat.

- If your pet touches the target and you missed an opportunity to click, just move on. It is better not to click than to click late.

- If you click by accident (your bunny did not really deserve it), you must give the treat anyway. A click means a treat—every time.

If you want to practice your clicker timing without confusing your rabbit, practice the timing of your clicks with the help of a training partner. Ask your partner to bounce a ball slowly. Practice clicking the moment the ball touches the ground. As your timing improves, ask your friend to speed up the bounces.

CHAPTER 4
What Should I Teach?

What inspired you to train your rabbit? Did you see a rabbit on TV or in a movie do something especially cute? Does a friend have a rabbit with an amazing repertoire of tricks? Do you want to get involved in the sport of Rabbit Hopping? Perhaps you just passed by this book in the store and were intrigued by the idea of training your rabbit.

Before choosing a trick to train, observe your pet. Watch his natural behavior and identify some things he does. For example, bunnies hop. Jumping over an obstacle, therefore, would be a great trick to teach a bunny, especially if your bunny seems to jump over anything and everything. Once your rabbit begins to respond to clicks and treats, and you become comfortable with the training process, you can teach any behavior your rabbit is physically capable of doing.

Rabbits love to jump. Once a bunny has learned the cue word 'jump' you can teach it to jump many kinds of obstacles.

CHOOSING SUITABLE TRICKS

Start by training something easy that your rabbit does without much prompting, then work up to more complicated or physically challenging tricks. Find your own rabbit's strengths and focus on tricks that emphasize those strengths. If your rabbit loves to jump, teach him to jump over bars and through hoops and on top of platforms. If he's especially paw oriented, teach him "Gimme Five" and "Gimme Ten," tricks in which he touches your hand.

Some tricks are more than cute behaviors taught just for fun. Tricks can be useful behaviors that make your rabbit's life with you easier. You can teach your bunny to sit still for nail trims, to allow you to medicate him, to use a litter box, or to come when you call him.

Clicker training can also solve behavior problems by replacing undesired behaviors with preferred ones. For example, if your bunny does not like to be picked up, you can click and treat him for allowing touching in various places until you can eventually pick him up. Rescued bunnies benefit greatly from training because it gives the new owner a positive strategy for coping with problems, and it gives the rabbit problem-solving skills and positive experiences to replace any unpleasant memories.

Many rabbits are nervous about being held or picked up. Katie can hold Angel gently for just a second, click, let go, give a treat, and then repeat the process, slowly adding a second or two each time, to build confidence in small steps.

GUIDELINES FOR TRAINING

In the next several chapters, we provide step-by-step instructions for teaching both fun tricks and useful behaviors and for solving some common behavior problems. Following are some tips for training sessions and a simple outline for training any behaviors. Although the behaviors you are trying to teach will change, the basic steps will not. If a trick you want to teach is not included in this book, you'll be able to use this outline to create your own training plan.

General Guidelines

- Do all steps in order without skipping any.

- Do at least ten repetitions at each step. If a certain step is difficult for your rabbit, do more. Do not do fewer than ten repetitions (you can spread them out over the course of several sessions).

- Don't worry about how much progress is made in a given session. As long as you and your pet are having fun and you've made a bit of progress, the session was a success.

- When you start a new session, start one step back from where you left off and repeat that step three times as a refresher.

- If your rabbit seems bored, use a more highly favored reward.

- Treat after every click.

- The click "ends" the behavior. After you click, your bunny is free to come to you for his treat.

- You do not have to perfect one trick before beginning

training another. If you want to switch to a different trick, however, move to a different location or wait until another session.

Manipulating the Environment

In order to be able to click a behavior and get your rabbit on the road to learning a new trick, you need to get him started in the right direction. Your rabbit will not be a happy learner if you push, pull, lift, carry, or otherwise use physical force to get him to do something. In fact if you try to force your rabbit, even gently, he will most likely turn his back on you, thump, hide, or go sulk in his cage.

The best way to get a rabbit started doing something click-able is to manipulate the training environment so that he is likely to go in the right direction on his own. Most rabbits are very attached to their litter box and you can use this to help teach your rabbit to do many things. Sitting in the litter box can be a reward in itself for a rabbit. You may wish to bring one or more litter boxes to the training area so that your rabbit feels very comfortable. You can take advantage of the rabbit's desire to sit in his litter box by putting an obstacle in between the bunny and the litter box; when he navigates the obstacle to get to the box, use the clicker to train that behavior.

Oreo jumps toward his familiar litter box. The "track" unrolled on the floor helps him keep going in the right direction.

For example, to teach a rabbit to jump, place the litter box at one end of your training mat. Position a low jump just before the litter box, and two barriers (shoe boxes would work) on either side of the jump. Place the rabbit between the boxes and he will most likely choose to go over the jump to get to the litter box. Click as he jumps and treat in the litter box. After a few successes you can remove the barriers and move the jump away from the litter box in small increments. Click and treat for every jump. Soon the rabbit will understand that the jumping gets a treat. Then you can add the cue "Jump" or a hand signal.

Because rabbits like to jump, this is an easy first trick to teach. When your rabbit gets to the point where he loves to jump over the jump, introduce another obstacle, a tunnel perhaps, just before the jump. Again, set barriers so that going through the tunnel is the only way he can get to the jump.

Rabbits also love to go into boxes. Cut a rabbit-sized hole in the bottom of one side of a two-foot-square box and place the box in the training area with your rabbit. He will almost certainly go into the box. Click when he goes in. When he hears the click, he will come out for the treat. Once he is enthusiastic about this in-and-out-of-the-box game, place an obstacle in front of the entrance to the box so that the rabbit must navigate the obstacle, perhaps a tunnel or another jump. You can gradually increase the distance from the obstacle to

"Hmm. I'm not sure what I'm supposed to do, here." This is a three-step behavior: go up the ramp, across the stool, and down the other ramp. Teaching the "down ramp" first would help the rabbit understand where to go next; or the trainer could use a target to show the rabbit where to go next to earn a click.

the box and click/treat the rabbit for navigating the obstacle. Eventually you can take the box away and your rabbit will still like to go through the tunnel or around the block, or whatever it is you used as an obstacle, because doing so is associated with something else he likes to do.

Use your imagination and your knowledge of the things your rabbit likes to do to teach him to go under, over, around, or through obstacles. Rabbits are capable of learning the difference between two actions, such as "under" and "over," and they can learn verbal cues to go over and under a specific object, such as a box or a bridge.

Training Outline

Although individual behaviors are as varied as the minds imagining them, the basic steps for teaching those behaviors are the same.

1. Get the behavior. A few ways to elicit behavior: Set up the environment so that the behavior is likely to happen and then click when the behavior does happen; guide your bunny through the trick with food or a target stick; or break the behavior down into more easily achievable baby steps and then "build" a more complex behavior. Click and reward the instant your bunny achieves what you are looking for at that moment.

2. Repeat until your bunny is actively and reliably offering that response.

3. Make the behavior a little more difficult by taking one baby step closer to the final trick. Repeat until your rabbit offers this new variation reliably, and then take another baby step.

4. When your rabbit is doing the complete trick, add a cue.

From that point on, click only cued performances of the trick.

5. If the trick requires your rabbit to perform the behavior for a period of time, begin to add duration now. Start with one second, and baby step by baby step, increase the amount of time he must perform before you click.

6. If the trick includes distance, add it now, in baby steps.

7. If you'd like your bunny to perform this trick in more than one location, begin taking the behavior "on the road." Initially, this might be as simple as moving the training environment a few feet away from where it normally is or perhaps orienting it differently. Then you can move to different rooms and eventually outside or to different buildings.

8. Using baby steps, accustom your bunny to working despite distractions. For example, you might want to teach your bunny to perform the trick in front of other people— perhaps even lots of other people.

TRAINING IN A NUTSHELL

1. Get the behavior the way you want it
2. Add the cue
3. Add duration
4. Add distance
5. Generalize to other locations
6. Add distractions

KEEP IT FUN!

Don't forget that this process is supposed to be fun for both you and your rabbit. Sometimes training sessions don't go the way we plan. Sometimes our pets don't progress the way we want them to. Sometimes we get confused ourselves or can't figure out exactly how to get what we want. That's okay.

If you get frustrated, end the session, and just play with your bunny for a little while. Hold him and stroke him and remember why you're doing this. If you feel like you're stuck, switch to a different trick, even a well-known one, for a while. Enjoy the journey as much as the destination. When your bunny amazes you with a perfect trick, give him an extra big treat and end the training session on a good note.

CHAPTER 5
Fun Tricks to Teach Your Rabbit

In this chapter you'll find specific recipes for training several fun tricks. Each recipe begins with a description of the desired behavior, followed by a list of instructions to teach your rabbit the behavior. (All of these recipes assume your pet is familiar with targeting—see "Basic Target Training" in Chapter 3, page 29.) These steps are guidelines. If you can think of other ways to get the behavior, feel free to use your imagination. Your bunny will actually become a better learner if you let him figure things out on his own; you don't have to use a lure or a target all the time. You can manipulate the environment and use props, as described in Chapter 4, page 35, to give your rabbit the best chance of doing what you want without you having to show him. Your bunny may even come up with things you didn't think of. Feel free to click and reward these creative efforts.

"Pick a card, any card." Who needs a magician? Oreo does his own magic tricks.

To help make training simple, we suggest specific verbal cues and hand signals. Again, these are just suggestions. Feel

DeeDee loves to retrieve her dumbbell for clicks and treats.

free to choose something completely different. Be sure to be consistent with your own bunny. Clicker training is all about creativity and partnership, so use your imagination, pay attention to your pet, and see where you end up!

STAND ON HIND LEGS (OR "SIT PRETTY")

Description: Your rabbit stands on his hind legs or sits up on his haunches.

1. Present the target about half an inch above your rabbit's nose. Click for touching the target. Remove the target, and give your bunny a treat.

2. Present the target about an inch above your rabbit's nose. Click for touching the target. Remove the target, and give your bunny a treat.

3. Continue to baby step the target higher and higher, increasing between half an inch and an inch at a time, until your rabbit will stand on his hind legs or sit on his haunches (whichever you prefer).

4. Next, when your bunny reliably performs the behavior, add a cue. Say your new cue, "Sit pretty," and then present the target stick. From this point, use the cue each time. Do not click and reward if your bunny does the behavior without hearing or seeing the cue first.

5. Begin adding duration. Cue the behavior, and then, after your bunny stands up, wait one second before clicking and rewarding.

6. Use baby steps to add more duration … two, three, four, or more seconds. Vary the number of seconds you ask your bunny to stand. Add duration slowly so he can build strength and balance.

7. Do several short (one second) repetitions of the behavior. Then verbally cue the behavior but don't present the target stick. If your rabbit offers the behavior, click and reward with several small treats.

"GIMME TEN"

Description: Your rabbit stands on his hind legs or sits on his haunches, then places both front paws on your fingers. (Use a flat, up-turned palm in this trick to differentiate it from "Gimme Five.")

1. Teach your bunny to stand or sit pretty on cue.

2. Cue your bunny to stand. Raise your hand, palm facing up, so that your hand comes up under his front paws. As soon as his paws touch your fingers, click and reward.

3. Cue your bunny to stand. Place your palm under his front feet but do not touch them. Wait until he touches your hand. Click and reward.

4. Add the cue to the new behavior: First, cue the stand. After your rabbit stands, but before presenting your hand, give the new cue, "Gimme Ten." Present your hand, and click and reward a touch.

5. After several quick repetitions, cue "Gimme Ten" and present your hand without first cueing the stand.

Little Ernie makes new friends by doing his "Gimme Ten" for a click and treat.

"GIMME FIVE"

Description: Your rabbit lifts one paw and "slaps" (targets) your finger. (Use a single finger for this trick to differentiate it from the up-turned palm in "Gimme Ten.")

1. Place your rabbit on a table (making sure he can't jump or fall off). Use your fingertip to touch one of his front feet. Eventually you want him to lift his foot and target your finger, so touch the side or front under the nail in a way that, with a little encouragement, he will be likely to lift his foot. Click and reward your bunny if he allows you to touch him. If your rabbit won't allow you to approach his foot, start over with smaller baby steps:

a. Reach out toward your rabbit's foot, but stop several inches away, before your bunny moves away. Click if your rabbit sits still. After you click, withdraw your finger, and give your rabbit a treat.

b. Baby step an inch, or even a half inch, at a time closer to his foot until you can touch it for just a moment. He has to sit still to earn a click and a treat.

2. Wiggle your finger against your rabbit's foot or nail to encourage him to lift it. Click the moment he touches your finger.

3. Present your finger target right in front of his foot. If he doesn't target it with his foot, prompt a bit by lightly touching his nail.

4. When he is actively touching your finger, use baby steps to teach him to target your finger when it is presented a little higher or a little farther away.

5. Add the cue, "Gimme five." Say the cue, and then present your finger target.

SIT IN A BASKET

Description: Your rabbit climbs into a basket and stays there. This is a great way to get your bunny to pose for cute photos. This trick can also be used to transport pets that do not like to be picked up, and it provides a good way for children to carry a rabbit safely. Choose a basket with low sides so your bunny can climb in easily but still be safe when being carried.

1. Place the basket on the floor of the training area near your bunny. Click him for sniffing or showing any interest in

the basket. Deliver the reward near the basket to encourage him to interact with it.

2. Use your target stick to guide your rabbit into the basket. Once inside, give several small treats in a row. Your rabbit will learn that inside this basket is a great place to be!

3. Add a cue, "Basket," to get your bunny to climb in the basket. Give the cue, then present your target stick in the middle of the basket to encourage him to climb in. When he starts climbing in, remove the target stick, and click him for four paws in the basket. Again, give several small treats in a row for being inside.

4. Use the verbal cue, "Basket," but don't present the target stick. Click your bunny for four paws in the basket.

5. Teach your bunny to stay in the basket. After he climbs in, wait one second before clicking.

6. Use baby steps to teach your bunny to stay in the basket longer and longer. As you progress, vary the amount of time you ask him to stay. One great way to get longer stays is to give your rabbit something to chew on during the stay. For example, put some hay in the basket. The more comfortable the basket, the easier it is to teach your rabbit to stay there.

7. Cue your rabbit to get into the basket. With him in it, lift the basket just a quarter inch. Click if your bunny holds still, and immediately set the basket down again.

8. Use baby steps to gradually increase the height of the lift until you are comfortably standing with the basket. Click

when the basket is in the air and your bunny is still. Reward by putting the basket down and giving a treat.

9. Lift your bunny in the basket and take one step. Click if your bunny remains still. Reward by putting the basket down and giving a treat.

10. Use baby steps to increase your rabbit's confidence until you can carry him around in his basket.

JUMP

Description: A bunny can jump in many ways. He can jump over a pole, through a hoop, onto a platform, or into a basket. This particular trick teaches your bunny to jump over a pole; with a few slight variations you can easily apply these steps to jumping in other situations. (Be certain that you train this trick on a non-slippery surface.)

1. Place a wooden dowel or other "bar" for jumping on the floor of the training area. Use your target stick to guide your rabbit over the bar. Click when the back feet go over the bar. Sometimes rabbits will jump over an object just because it is there. Terrific! Click at the height of the jump.

2. Raise one end of the bar about an inch. Use the target stick to lead your rabbit across, clicking when the back feet go over the bar, or, click when he jumps on his own.

3. Set both ends of the jump about one inch off the ground, and click for crossing it. To avoid a risk of injury, make sure the bar will fall if it's bumped by your rabbit, but don't click if he knocks over the bar.

4. Use baby steps to raise the bar to the point that your rabbit is jumping over it, rather than just stepping.

5. Add a cue, "Jump." Give the cue, then present the target stick, if necessary, on the other side.

6. If you're still using the target stick, fade it from the picture. Give the verbal cue, but don't present the target stick. Click your bunny for jumping the bar.

7. Place your rabbit a few inches farther away from the jump. Give the "Jump" cue.

8. Use baby steps to add distance between your rabbit and the jump.

Fuzzzy learned to go over jumps on cue, for a click and treat. Now he'll jump anything, even a water jump complete with ducks.

SPIN

Description: In this trick, your rabbit turns in a circle to the left. You can also train your bunny to turn in a circle to the right, but teach it as a separate trick, and give it a different cue.

1. Present a target stick in front and slightly to the left of your rabbit. Click any movement of a paw in the direction of the spin.

2. Present the target stick an inch or two farther back, so your bunny has to turn a bit more to touch it. Click the turn.

3. Progressing in baby steps, use your target stick to guide your bunny through a full turn.

4. When your rabbit is reliably turning a full circle, add the cue, "Spin." Say the cue, then use your target stick to guide your bunny through the behavior.

5. Fading the physical prompt for this behavior can be tricky. One baby step to make it easier is to fade the target stick and use just the hand movement. Then use baby steps to make the hand signal more and more subtle, finally using only the verbal cue.

GOAL!

Description: Here, you teach your rabbit to push a ball with his nose through two "goal posts."

Rolling a ball is a game many rabbits enjoy. Once your bunny learns to play, if you leave a ball in his area he may push it around on his own just

Goal! Blackie is a good soccer player and know how to push the ball through the goal posts.

for fun. A variation on this trick is to roll a ball to your bunny and have him roll it back to you.

1. Place two cones about a foot apart in the training area. These will be your goal posts. Put the ball on the floor between the posts and right in front of your bunny. Click when your bunny's nose touches the ball. Remove the ball after clicking, and give your bunny a treat.

2. When your bunny is reliably touching the ball, begin watching the ball's movement. Position the ball so if it rolls half an inch, it will be "through" the goal posts. Click when the bunny pushes the ball one-half inch through the posts.

3. Use baby steps to increase the distance your bunny must push the ball to get it through the posts.

4. Add a verbal cue, "Goal." Give the cue, and then put the ball down. Click when the ball rolls through the goal posts.

PUTTING TRICKS TOGETHER

Doing tricks one at a time is fun, but the creative opportunities are endless if you combine the tricks into sequences. One of the tricks in the previous section, "Gimme Ten," is actually a simple sequence of two of your rabbit's behaviors—standing on his back legs and targeting your hand with his front feet.

A good way to use sequences of behaviors is to create an obstacle course. If your bunny can jump over a jump, go through a tunnel, and follow a target stick, you can set up all sorts of courses in your house or yard. The obstacles can be almost anything as long as they are rabbit-sized and rabbit-safe. Make your own obstacles from things around the house or from the hardware store. If you don't mind your bunny doing ninety miles an hour through your house, show him how to go over, under, and through the furniture as an obstacle course.

There is an official obstacle-course sport for rabbits, called Rabbit Hopping. Rabbits compete against each other over a series of jumps, as horses do. Rabbits also compete in the high jump and long jump. (You can find out all about Rabbit Hopping on at the website www.kaninhop.dk/uk.) You can also have fun with your rabbit by making small obstacles like those used in dog agility competitions. These may include jumps, weave poles, tunnels, an A-frame, or a balance beam.

Before you try to perform multiple tricks in a row, teach the behaviors individually. Get them on cue and strong. When

Angel goes through two tunnels, one after the other, and gets a click at the end.

you begin to work on a sequence, you want your bunny to be thinking about performing, not trying to figure out how to do the basic behaviors.

For your first sequence, pick just two behaviors, Behavior A and Behavior B. Begin by cueing Behavior B several times, each repetition followed with a favorite reward. Get your bunny excited about performing Behavior B. Then give the cue for Behavior A. As your rabbit performs Behavior A, give him the cue for Behavior B (which he was just so excited about performing). Click the completion of Behavior B and reward him with several small, very special treats.

Repeat the sequence in the opposite direction (A to B). Begin with several repetitions of Behavior A, then reward Behavior A with the cue for B. Mix and match other pairs of behaviors using the same technique. It won't take many two-behavior sequences for your bunny to catch on to the idea that two behaviors in a row is just part of the game and is worth a great reward. After you sequence together two behaviors, you're ready to try three. Then four. Then five. The sky is the limit!

CHAPTER 6
Useful Tricks

Rabbits need care to keep them healthy and happy, care that goes beyond fresh food and water. They need their cages cleaned. They need to get used to being handled and examined. They need their nails trimmed and their bodies groomed. If your bunny gets sick, he may need to take pills, have medicine put in his eyes or ears, sit still for an injection, or allow the vet to examine him. Clicker training can help make all these things easier for you and less stressful for your pet.

This chapter presents step-by-step recipes for various tricks that are more than just fun: The behaviors your rabbit will learn when practicing these tricks will be useful in everyday life.

Oreo first learned to accept being petted, held, and carried for clicks and treats. Now he truly enjoys snuggling with his favorite human.

COME WHEN CALLED

Description: Your rabbit comes to you when you give him the cue to "Come."

This behavior, also called "recall," provides a foundation for other training and is useful for all pets to know. Friends and family will be impressed when your bunny comes when you call him, and you will be relieved to not have to chase him around the house for half an hour when it's time for bed! (See "Tips for Great Recalls" on page 57.)

1. Clear the training area of all distractions. Sit on the floor with your bunny about a foot away from you. Click your bunny for looking toward you or for taking a step toward you. Deliver an especially wonderful treat on the floor right in front of you.

2. Same setup, but click only when your bunny comes to you.

3. Begin to add the cue, "Come." As your bunny hops to you, give the cue.

4. Give the verbal cue just before your bunny hops toward you.

5. Use baby steps to slowly add distance. Always use an especially good treat.

6. Begin training the behavior in other locations. When you go to a new location, start all the way back at Step 1. You may progress quickly through the steps—or you may not, especially if there are a lot of distractions. Don't rush; be patient.

TIPS FOR GREAT RECALLS

- Click and reward your bunny for "checking in"—voluntarily coming to you when he is out of his cage.

- Reward all recalls!

- If you're going to do something your bunny won't like, such as putting him back in his cage or trimming his nails, don't call him to you. Go and get him.

- If your bunny is hopping away from you, and you aren't 100 percent sure he will respond to the recall cue, don't use it. Go get him. Save the cue for times when you're sure he will respond, until he always comes gladly.

- Do lots and lots of recalls with clicks and treats... and then let him go play again. He learns that coming to you means something good happens, and it doesn't necessarily mean the fun is going to end.

- If you have tried to teach a recall previously, and your rabbit ignores the cue, pick a different cue and start teaching the behavior from scratch.

GO HOME

Description: Your bunny goes into his cage, house, or carrier on cue.

This is another foundation behavior that all pets can learn. A rabbit that will go into a cage or carrier on cue can easily be put to bed, taken to the vet, or gathered up in an emergency.

Your bunny can learn that "Go home" means go into

Teach your bunny to go in and out of his cage, carrier, and other enclosures on cue. Then he will be easier to catch and to transport.

whatever enclosure or container you offer. When training this behavior, however, you should start with an enclosure that your bunny likes to go into. This can be his cage, a pet carrier, or a box with an entryway cut into it. (If your bunny just came out of his cage, he may not want to go right back into it.) Set yourself up to succeed by choosing an enclosure he won't balk at entering.

1. Clear the training area of distractions. Place the enclosure on the floor near your bunny. Click for any interest in—sniffing or approach of—the enclosure. Give your rabbit the treat just inside the door of the enclosure.

2. Click your rabbit for going into the enclosure. You may, at first, click for only part of his body going in, but if you can toss the treat inside, he will be more and more willing to venture in.

3. When your rabbit is eagerly going into his enclosure, add the cue, "Go home." Start by saying the cue as he goes in.

4. Say the cue just before your bunny starts to enter the enclosure.

5. Say the cue, and click after your bunny goes into the enclosure. Feed the treat inside. While your bunny eats his treat, shut the door. Leave it closed for one second, and then open it again.

6. Use baby steps to increase the amount of time that the door is closed. Giving an especially good treat or putting something to chew on inside the enclosure will make your bunny happier about staying inside.

7. Place your bunny a foot farther from the enclosure, and then give him the cue to "Go home."

8. Use baby steps to increase the distance between your rabbit and the enclosure.

9. Change the enclosure's location. When you go to a new place, start with your bunny right next to the enclosure, and build distance slowly.

10. If you're going to use the "Go home" cue to put your bunny back in his cage for the night, give him some hay or a small handful of tiny treats to savor after he's inside.

LITTER BOX TRAINING

Description: Your rabbit consistently uses his litter box.

Rabbits naturally prefer to use a particular place for a toilet area. Many bunnies seem to lose this tendency when kept in a small cage with no different areas for different purposes, or when kept in a cage with a large number of other animals. Litter box training is well worth the effort, however, both for the health and comfort of your rabbit and also for your convenience. If your rabbit uses a litter box, then it is easy to monitor his health based on his potty habits. A litter box also means you'll have to clean the cage as a whole less frequently, which cuts down on cleaning chores and saves money on bedding.

The easiest way to begin litter box training is simply to put a litter box in the corner of your bunny's cage. He may start using it on his own. If not, follow these steps to teach him to use the box reliably.

DOES YOUR LITTER BOX PASS MUSTER?

Bunnies will use a litter box only if it meets their approval. These tips will make it more likely that your rabbit will give a passing grade to the litter box you offer.

- Your bunny must be able to get into and out of the box easily.

- The box must be placed in a location he considers suitable as a toilet. Many bunnies prefer a corner location for the litter box.

- The box must contain litter that he likes to use.

- The litter material cannot be the same material as his bedding.

- The litter material must be safe. Safe litter materials are listed at **www.rabbit.org/journal1/liver-disease.html.**

1. Set up your rabbit's cage environment to help him be successful. Remove everything from the cage. Feed from a rack attached to the side of the cage, and give water through a sipper bottle. Cover the entire bottom of the cage with the litter material. If possible place multiple litter boxes to cover the entire cage floor surface. Position the hay rack and sipper bottle over the place you think the rabbit is most likely to choose as a favorite litter box place (usually this would be in a corner).

2. After one week, put bedding in one quarter of the cage, and litter in the other three quarters. Put an actual litter box in one corner. Put a little used litter in the box to communicate the box's use. If you had placed multiple litter boxes in the cage, remove one of them and cover the area with bedding. If you catch your rabbit using the litter box, click and reward him!

3. If you find your rabbit prefers using a different area of his cage, change the location of the litter box to suit him. You may need to experiment with types of litter and bedding as well.

4. After another week, increase the ratio of bedding to litter on the cage floor or remove another of the extra litter boxes. Approximately half of the cage should have bedding in it, and half should have litter. The litter box should be in a corner with litter around it. Continue rewarding your bunny any time you catch him using the litter box. If you are very observant and have a high-value treat always at the ready, you can teach your bunny to "Go pee" on cue by clicking and treating when you catch him in the act and then adding the cue.

5. The following week, you may be able to line the entire cage in bedding and keep litter only in the box. However, if your bunny is not using the litter box reliably, use baby steps to reduce the amount of litter on the cage floor gradually. Many rabbits prefer to have two litter boxes, one predominantly for a toilet and one to sleep in and use as a toilet.

6. Once your rabbit is using a litter box reliably, you can put toys and other play areas back into the cage.

7. When you take your bunny out of his cage, take the litter box out as well, so that he always has access to it. Click and reward him for choosing the box. Take the litter box wherever you take the rabbit. Rabbits can learn to look for and use their own litter box in a new place, so your friends will be happy to have you and your furry friend visit!

HOUSE TRAINING VS. MARKING

Some rabbit owners are frustrated by "accidents" outside the litter box with pets that seem to be fully litter box trained. If your bunny uses the litter box reliably nearly all the time, but sometimes urinates or defecates around the house or occasionally in other parts of the cage, this is probably marking behavior, rather than an accident.

Some rabbits are territorial, and they may be staking out new territory by marking, or their marking behavior may be triggered by anxiety or by the smell of another pet. If you have two rabbits and you let one out to run around the living room, all may be well. But if you then let the other rabbit out, you may find droppings all over the room as the second bunny responds to the presence of the first. Rabbits also leave droppings to help them navigate and find their way back if they wander far from their home area.

Neutering or spaying your bunny may help if urine marking is a problem and you want your pet to have free run of the house. Talk about this with a veterinarian who specializes in small animals.

CAGE CLEANING

Description: Your bunny stays calm while you reach into his cage to clean it, or he allows you to pick him up and take him out of the cage when it's time for cleaning.

Every bunny's cage should be cleaned regularly, but this is stressful for some rabbits. Imagine how you would feel if you had just spent a week messing up your room to the perfect state of comfort and smelliness and along comes a giant hand, scooping out all your work and forcing you to start over again! Some rabbits do not like hands invading their cages. Some are afraid, and others are just trying to get a good day's sleep! All of these scenarios lead to bunnies who are grumpy when you try to clean their cages.

You can teach your bunny to sit still and remain relaxed when you reach in and pick him up. You could also teach him a cue to come out of the cage on his own, or to go into a different enclosure temporarily. If you do take him out of his cage while you clean it, give him something fun and entertaining to do while you clean, so he will look forward to the experience.

1. Teach your bunny to sit quietly or to approach happily when you open the cage door. Use baby steps if your bunny is uncomfortable when you reach for the cage door:

   a. Approach the cage. If your bunny sits quietly or eagerly approaches the front of the cage, click and offer a treat through the bars. If he lays back his ears, growls, or gets restless, stop moving and wait. When he visibly relaxes a tiny bit, click and offer a treat through the bars. Then back away.

   b. When your bunny is relaxed with your approach, reach toward the door. Stop without touching the door. Click if your bunny is calm. If your bunny reacts negatively, freeze. Wait until your bunny relaxes a tiny bit, and then move your hand away. Reach more slowly next time and stop before your bunny reacts.

   c. Use baby steps to touch, and then open, the cage door.

2. Open the cage door and reach a short distance inside. If your bunny stays relaxed, click. Drop a treat inside, and then remove your hand. If you're worried that your rabbit might bite you, wear gloves until he has associated the presence of your hand with good things for bunnies. If he does bite, you don't want to reward him by removing your hand. Remove your hand only when he relaxes a bit.

3. Reach toward and touch your bunny. Again, click relaxed acceptance, and after you give the treat, take your hand away.

4. Use baby steps to teach your bunny that being touched and finally picked up results in lots of good things. Be sure to support his back legs when you lift him, so he feels secure.

NAIL CLIPPING

Description: Your rabbit allows you to hold him and clip his nails.

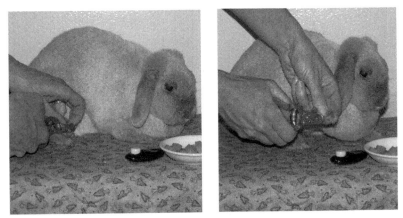

a: Trimming back foot toenails   b: Trimming front foot toenails.

This rabbit has learned to sit patiently and allow his nails to be clipped, on all four feet, for a click and treat. The i-Click clicker can be pressed with your foot to keep your hands free.

Any animal that does not wear down its nails needs to have them clipped, and that includes your pet bunny. Nails that are not clipped can be torn off or curl under, leading to deformed toes. Long nails can scratch people or other pets. Unfortunately, trimming nails is a task that all too frequently is considered torturous by both human and rabbit. One rabbit made it very clear that there was to be no more nail clipping by taking his handler's index finger in his mouth and glaring at her.

Fortunately, you can clicker train your bunny to make nail clipping easier for both of you. This is a complex behavior. Your bunny might fly through some steps and take weeks with others. That's all right. Progress only when your bunny is comfortable and convinced that you're not going to hurt him. You may find it difficult to hold a clicker, treats, nail clipper, and your rabbit. Working with an assistant who can handle the clicker and treats is helpful. If you're working solo, try making a click sound with your mouth or position a type of clicker with a protruding button, called an i-Click, under your foot so that you can click without using your hand.

1. Lift your bunny and position him on your lap so you can hold him close and handle his feet. If necessary, use baby steps to teach him to allow you to lift him and hold him close. Be sure to support his back legs, so he feels secure when you lift him. Don't progress until he can sit quietly when held tightly in your arms for at least thirty seconds.

2. Pick up one of his feet. Touch the toes. Touch the nails. Lightly squeeze the toes. Restrain his foot for a few seconds. You may have to teach each of these steps in individual baby steps. That's fine! Using lots of baby steps means lots of rewards, which means your rabbit will quickly learn that this game is not a threat.

3. Repeat for each foot.

4. Pick up a foot, and show your bunny the clippers. If your bunny has a "history" with the clippers he may react at just the sight of them. If so, stop and use baby steps. Put the clippers on a nearby table while you handle your bunny's feet and click and reward. Gradually move the clippers

closer until you're able to show them to your bunny without an emotional reaction.

5. Hold a foot and touch one nail with the clippers. Just touch. Don't clip. Click during each touch and treat afterward. Use baby steps to tap all of his nails.

6. Clip a wooden match or a twig or flower stem with the nail clippers. Let your bunny get used to the sound.

7. Hold one foot, and clip the end off a single nail. Release your bunny and have a little party with lots of tiny treats. Clip one nail a day until you've clipped each nail one time.

8. Clip two nails, clicking and heavily rewarding after each. Clip two nails a day until you've clipped all his nails.

9. Clip three nails and so on, until you're able to trim all of his nails in a single session.

GROOMING

Description: Your rabbit does not protest when you groom him.

Most rabbits benefit from regular grooming, even if it is just a wipe down with a damp cloth to remove loose fur. The best time to groom your pet is when he is sleepy or mentally tired after a clicker training session. You may end up in a wrestling match if you try to groom him when he is feeling frisky and wants to run and play.

1. Lift your bunny and position him on your lap so you can hold him close and handle his body. If necessary, use baby steps to teach him to allow you to lift him and hold him close. Be sure to support his back legs, so he feels secure when you lift him. Don't progress until he can sit quietly when held tightly in your arms for at least thirty seconds.

2. Touch his entire body—ears, face, feet, belly. You may have to teach each body part in individual baby steps. That's fine! Using lots of baby steps means lots of rewards, which means your rabbit will quickly learn that this game is not a threat.

3. Introduce the grooming tools. You may be able only to show him the towel or brush initially. Use baby steps to teach him to let you touch and stroke him with the tools.

HANDLING AND VETERINARY CARE

Rabbits are naturally social and can learn to enjoy your company and being handled. The more you can handle your bunny and provide a positive experience during handling, the more he will come to enjoy being handled. If you have to take your rabbit to the vet one day, it will be much less stressful for him and everyone else if he calmly accepts being transported in a cage or basket and being handled and lifted.

• For more information on teaching your bunny to ride in a basket, see "Sit in a Basket" on page 17.

• To teach your rabbit to go inside an enclosure, see "Go Home" on page 57.

• To teach your bunny to accept being lifted and handled, refer to "Grooming" on page 66.

CHAPTER 7
Solving Problem Behavior

Clicker training is good for more than just tricks and health care; the clicker also can help you solve behavior problems. Clicking builds a foundation of trust that counteracts any behavioral issues, such as fear or aggression, that your rabbit may have. For a clicker trainer with a "clicker-wise" rabbit, fixing behavior problems involves the same process as teaching a trick. No matter what you're trying to teach, your rabbit will love to hear that clicker and will be eager to work with you. For the truly clicker-wise bunny, the mere sight of you with the clicker will make him feel positive and happy.

FREQUENTLY ASKED QUESTIONS

Many pet behavior problems involve behaviors that, though troublesome to the pet owner, may have an instinctive basis in the pet. Understanding what's behind your rabbit's behavior helps when working to eliminate problem behaviors. Also, as when you are training tricks, it's important to carefully observe your rabbit; you'll want to be able to identify and immediately "click" the good behavior. In this chapter, we look at questions commonly asked by rabbit owners about specific problem behaviors and offer suggestions on how to use the clicker to work with your rabbit to eliminate the unwanted behavior.

How can I teach my rabbit not to attack my hand when I clean his cage?

Use the clicker to create a positive association with your hand coming into the cage. Click and treat through the bars of the cage at first. Gradually place your hand closer and closer to the door of the cage as you click and treat. Open the cage and click and treat, dropping the treats in or feeding through the bars. Place your hand at the open cage door. Click and treat for any movement toward your hand that is not aggressive. Start giving the treats from your hand at the cage door, gradually moving your hand farther in until your rabbit is taking the treats from your hand.

You could also use a target stick to teach your bunny to come out of the cage on cue. Then you would not have to put your hand into the cage until after your rabbit has come out.

Sweet Pea, who doesn't know Jennifer very well, has let himself be picked up for a click and treat. Rabbits hate to feel their legs dangling, so Jennifer is careful to support his front legs with one hand and his hind legs with the other so he feels more secure.

My rabbit only likes my sister. How can I get him to like me too?

Everyone has preferences—even our pets! Clicker training is a great way to create a positive relationship with more than one person. Teach your rabbit a few tricks that she can do with several people, and she will certainly look at other people in a more favorable light, knowing that they are a source of fun and food.

How can I stop my rabbit from biting?

Sometimes rabbits bite when trying to see if something is edible. Usually, however, rabbits bite people because biting gets people to leave them alone. Try to recognize the situations that trigger biting and the body language that signals a bite is about to happen. For example, a bunny that freezes and lays its ears back may be getting ready to bite. Think about what's been going on that causes him to get to this state, and see if you can avoid these triggers.

Each time you play with your rabbit, do some clicker training; this will keep him occupied and help distract him from any biting triggers. Doing lots of repetitions of easy behavior with a high rate of success will keep your rabbit so busy, he won't have time to even think about biting. If he does bite you, try not to react. Hitting or yelling will not help; it will make the situation worse. If your rabbit is biting to make you go away, then putting him down will actually be rewarding him and will make the behavior worse.

Do not pick up or touch a rabbit that bites. Teach him to accept touching and hands in his cage using the clicker method by slowly introducing hands and touching while clicking and treating. Teach him to get in a basket or carrying case for clicks and treats. (See the training recipes in Chapters 5 and 6 for more information on training your rabbit to accept handling and being carried.)

To teach your bunny to take treats carefully and not nip fingers by accident, use soft treats such as mashed banana and click for licking.

Teach your rabbit to be careful around your hands: Smear a little banana on a spoon or dowel. Click while the rabbit licks off the banana. Take the object away briefly if he bites. Once you are sure that the rabbit knows to lick rather than bite at the smeared banana, you can put some on your finger and teach the rabbit to lick you rather than bite. Sweet Pea, who doesn't know Jennifer very well, has let himself be picked up, for a click and treat. Rabbits hate to feel their legs dangling, so Jennifer is careful to support his front legs with one hand and his hind legs with the other so he feels more secure.

Sometimes my rabbit urinates on guests. How can I stop this?

Sometimes a bunny just has to go! They may wriggle and squirm or dig to try to get to a more appropriate spot, but if they can't, then there may be an accident. Learn your rabbit's body language, so you can give him a potty break when he needs it.

In other cases, a bunny may be afraid or has learned from past experience that he will be let go if he pees on people. The solution to this problem is to let your rabbit adjust first to the new person before picking him up or letting the new person pick him up. Sit on the floor and click and treat if he investigates or comes close. Don't rush him. Teach him that great things happen when new people are around. Place him in his litter box just before a new person handles him or if you think he may be anxious. You can even teach him to pee on cue (in his litter box, not on a guest!) by capturing the behavior with a click and treats, and then giving a cue.

*My rabbit seems lonely. Is it a good idea to get another
bunny for company?*

Rabbits are social creatures and benefit from the company of
other rabbits. If you think your pet could use a friend, you are
probably right. Same-sex siblings are often good companions,
but sometimes they fight as they mature. You may need to spay
or neuter them. Many bunnies in shelters are waiting for a new
home, so check there first when looking for a new rabbit. Some
shelters have begun including clicker training programs for rabbits. Shelter rabbits may be accustomed to the noise, activity,
and other animals in the shelter so they are not afraid of general
household hubbub and can fit quickly into a busy family.

There is a popular myth that guinea pigs can be good companions for rabbits, but it's not a good idea. Guinea pigs need
to eat more fresh greens in their diet than rabbits do; too many
greens may cause stomach problems for rabbits. Rabbits can
hurt a small guinea pig with their powerful hind legs. Some
rabbits may try to mate with a guinea pig and cause injury.

When you get a new companion for your bunny, the
following steps will help them learn to be friends. This all-
positive method has been dubbed the "bunnymoon." It can be
used to introduce a new pet to the household or to bond pets
that are initially hostile to each other.

1. Put the two pets in separate cages. Position the cages across
   the room from each other so the rabbits can see each other
   but have no physical contact. Click and reward them for
   looking at each other without showing signs of aggression.
   Click each time you put food into the cage of each rabbit.

2. Over a period of several days, use baby steps to move the
   cages closer. Continue to click and treat for calm or friend-

ly interest. It could take weeks or months for the rabbits to tolerate each other. A hostile rabbit will turn his ears backward and lay them flat along his back. A rabbit with one ear up and one ear down is also indicating displeasure, but not outright hostility. Be patient and do not move on until both rabbits seem content in the separate (but not touching) cages.

3. Next, work with one bunny outside his cage and the other one inside his cage. Give them bowls of pellets and click and treat if they look at each other or touch each other through the bars. Give each rabbit a turn being inside or outside his own cage.

4. Switch litter boxes to allow the bunnies a chance to get to know each other's scent.

5. The next step is to switch the bunnies so that each one spends time in the other's enclosure, separately. Click and treat if they look at each other. Click and give a special treat if a rabbit is eating nicely in the other's cage.

6. Move the cages closer until the rabbits can touch noses through the bars. Give them pellets in their food bowls side by side in the separate cages. Click and treat for any looking, approaching, or touching through the bars that seems friendly. Use high-value treats. Between sessions, move the cages apart.

7. When the rabbits can touch each other without laying their ears back, let them meet on neutral territory outside the cages in another room. Put both litter boxes nearby so each rabbit has a familiar place to go for security. Give each rabbit a bowl of pellets. Let them eat side by side

for a few minutes, and then separate them to let them finish. Click and treat for any type of behavior that is calm or friendly.

Keep the sessions short (a few seconds at first) and do this several times until you are sure that the rabbits are not going to fight. Then allow the sessions to go on longer so that the bunnies can interact after they eat their meal. Play a few clicker games with them using well-rehearsed behaviors (such as coming when called) to help distract them from each other and keep them in a happy emotional state. Smear some banana on the inside of each bunny's ear for the other to lick off. This may cause them to groom each other. Once they do that, they will start to be friends.

8. When the rabbits have completed most of the steps above, don't be surprised if one bunny "mounts" the other. This may lead to a bit of a chase and some light fur pulling. If one or the other bunny pins his ears back and the chasing gets frantic or is accompanied by lunging and growling, call the bunnies to you, click and treat, and end the session. If your bunnies are well conditioned to come to you, they will be relieved to have a reason to stop the pre-fight behavior.

There is no need to stop the mounting and chasing behavior if it does not include lunging, growling, and pinned-back ears. Soon the mounting will decrease and one bunny will lie flat while being mounted. This is a sure sign that the bonding process has begun. It may still take several weeks or more for the rabbits to come to bond completely and be ready to live together in one cage.

9. Once they have begun to show that they like each other and can interact in neutral territory, you can try putting the

rabbits in the cage they will share. This enclosure must be large enough for each of them to be able to have space away from the other. A multilevel "condo" is a good arrangement, with several litter boxes in different areas. A brand-new cage is ideal, but if that's not practical, clean the existing cage thoroughly with a product designed to eliminate urine smell, and rearrange the furniture so that the original bunny resident is less likely to become territorial.

How can I stop my rabbit from chewing constantly on the bars of his cage?

Chewing is important for bunnies; it serves the purpose of keeping their teeth worn down. Chewing may also relieve stress and boredom, so it often becomes a habit. Punishment will not work to prevent chewing; it will increase anxiety in your rabbit, probably causing him to chew even more. Some people unintentionally reinforce bar chewing behavior by paying attention to their rabbit while he chews on the bars.

The good news is that because chewing on cage bars is a learned behavior, it can be unlearned as well.

Start by giving your bunny more appropriate things to chew on. Apple twigs, wooden chew blocks (not pine or cedar), unpainted wicker, and hay are all suitable for chewing. Introduce these things either in or out of the cage, and click and treat for any interest in chewing them. Apply some banana or other tasty treat to the item to stimulate your bunny's interest in chewing.

Another strategy for distracting your rabbit and creating focus away from chewing the bars is to scatter pelleted food throughout the cage rather than feeding the rabbit from a bowl. Your pet will be busy searching for the food and will enjoy chewing when he finds the pellets. Adding toys, new boxes, a climbing apparatus, or other enriching activities to the cage may help give your rabbit other things to do besides chew the bars. Providing your bunny with a larger and more interesting cage and/or moving the cage to an area in the house where he can see other pets and people coming and going may also help. Giving your rabbit more attention and time out of the cage for clicker training sessions is another way to help solve the bar chewing problem.

My rabbit is a chewing machine! Whenever he is out of his cage, he chews wires, furniture, you name it. How can I prevent this?

Jean Silva, a director of B.U.N.S, a rabbit rescue program in California, says that rabbits are given to us to smooth out the sharp edges of our lives—and our furniture! The best way to prevent chewing on wires or other dangerous or destructive chewing is to "bunny proof" the room your rabbit is allowed to run loose in. Here are some bunny-proofing tips from B.U.N.S.:

- Tack wires along the base of walls and install wire covers that can't be chewed through.

- Unplug any wires that cannot be protected.

- Install plastic corner guards on the exposed corners of walls. Rub soap on the corners of furniture.

- Place tubes along walls and behind furniture that rabbits can use as safe, wire-free paths around the room.

  Create a "sweet spot" in a room where many good things happen for a bunny that stays there. Provide chewable items in the sweet spot. Let your rabbit find hidden treats in allowed areas. Bunnies love a treasure hunt! Click and treat when your pet is in the sweet spot. Place a mat in the allowed area and click and treat whenever your rabbit is on the mat. This will help condition him to spend more and more time there. Place ramps, tunnels, and boxes there, and click and treat your rabbit for exploring these.

You will still need to supervise, but if you make it more rewarding for your rabbit to stay in the middle of a room or in an area away from wires or prized furniture, he will spend less and less time in the danger zones and more and more time in the sweet spot where all good things happen.

Mattie was once an unwanted pet. Now she's a bunny agility star of the B.U.N.S rabbit rescue center at the Santa Barbara County Animal Shelter in California.

CHAPTER 8

Where to Learn More

We hope you'll try a few of our recipes for training your rabbit fun and useful tricks. Even more so, we hope *Clicking with Your Rabbit* will help you develop a closer relationship with your rabbit, so you can have many happy years together. If you would like to learn more about clicker training or rabbit behavior and care, the following resources are a good place to start.

IMPROVING YOUR CLICKER TIMING AND TECHNIQUE

- Timing games you can play with your family and friends: **www.tagteach.com/games_drills.htm**

- Practice clicking this virtual bird and see how the number of rewards affects its behavior: **www.uwm.edu/~johnchay/oc.htm**

- Really want to learn clicker training? "Sniffy the Virtual Rat" lets you learn and practice both basic and advanced concepts: **http://tinyurl.com/a4kya**

CLICKER TRAINING INFORMATION AND GEAR

Karen Pryor's Clicker Training
A huge, ever-increasing collection of information on clicker training all kinds of animals. Includes a store with a wide selection of clicker training books, videos, and supplies: www.clickertraining.com.

INFORMATION ABOUT RABBIT CARE

House Rabbit Society
Lots of information about housing, health, litter box training, and nutrition of rabbits: www.rabbit.org.

The Language of Lagomorphs
A fascinating website about rabbit body language: www.muridae.com/rabbits/rabbittalk.html.

Carrot Café
A comprehensive guide explaining what to feed your rabbit, what foods to avoid, and how to help a rabbit with digestive problems: www.carrotcafe.com.

Bedding and Liver Disease
Important information for rabbit and small pet owners about many types of bedding and litter and the dangers of pine and cedar shavings: www.rabbit.org/journal/1/liver-disease.html.

Bunnies Urgently Needing Shelter (B.U.N.S.)
Rescue organization for bunnies and small pets. Includes lots of good information on care: www.bunssb.org.

CLICKER TRAINING DISCUSSION LISTS

The following e-mail discussion lists are great places to meet other clicker trainers and to ask questions about clicker training your bunny.

Clicker Bunny and Critters
A group for beginner and expert trainers dedicated to the discussion and development of clicker training approaches for small pets. Owned by animal behavior specialist Teresa Lewin, co-author of this book: **http://groups.yahoo.com/group/clickerbunnyandcritters**.

ClickerSolutions
A beginner-friendly website and discussion list for trainers of dogs and other animals, owned by Melissa Alexander, author of *Click for Joy*: **www.clickersolutions.com**.

Click-l
The original clicker list and website, with a huge membership and close monitoring to stay on topic: **www.click-l.com**.

Made in the USA
Charleston, SC
29 April 2010